HIS NAME IS WONDERFUL

DAILY READINGS FOR ADVENT FROM ISAIAH

2017 Edition

WIPF & STOCK · Eugene, Oregon

Mathew Bartlett

Wipf and Stock Publishers
199 W 8th Ave, Suite 3
Eugene, OR 97401

His Name is Wonderful
Daily Readings for Advent from Isaiah
By Bartlett, Mathew
Copyright©2017 Apostolos
ISBN 13: 978-1-5326-6869-2
Publication date 9/15/2018
Previously published by Apostolos, 2017

Week One: Sin, Confession, and Forgiveness
Sunday 3rd December: *The Problem to be Addressed*

> *Hear me, you heavens! Listen, earth! For the Lord has spoken: "I reared children and brought them up, but they have rebelled against me.... They have forsaken the Lord; they have spurned the Holy One of Israel and turned their backs on him. (Isaiah 1:2, 4)*

Well, this doesn't seem a positive way to begin our advent readings! In fact, the opening lines of Isaiah's prophecy appear rather bleak. Here is the picture which Isaiah paints: God's people have turned away from him. Despite continuing with their religious observances, their unholy actions in daily life proved that they had in fact become alienated from God.

Yet it is only by addressing the problem that Isaiah can deliver his message of hope. Just as a doctor must be clear about a patient's diagnosis before effective treatment can begin, so God requires us to admit our sins as a prelude to receiving his forgiveness.

On this first day of advent, it is helpful to begin our preparations for Christmas by examining our hearts. As the angel Gabriel announced the birth of Jesus, he declared 'you shall call his name Jesus for he shall save his people from their sins.' If we have sins to confess, then we should not become discouraged. We are among the blessed—for we are the ones that Jesus came to save! Take some time to confess your sins and accept God's promise of forgiveness, before worshipping the one who came to bring us hope and a fresh start with God.

> **Prayer:** Lord, on this first day of Advent, we confess our sins and failures to you. We thank you that you are gracious and willing to forgive. Hear our prayer as we examine our hearts and make ourselves ready to celebrate the time when hope—in the person of your son Jesus—came into the world. Amen.

Advent Reading Plan Day One: Isaiah 1:1–9; Mark 1:1–4.

Monday 4th December: *Come to Me–Hear Me–Listen to Me*

> *"Hear me, you heavens! Listen, earth! ... Hear the word of the Lord, ... listen to the instruction of our God ... (Isaiah 1:2, 10)*

Advent is a time of beginnings, and although the birth of Jesus is not foretold until chapter 7, Isaiah appears here to set the stage for Christmas by first highlighting *why* Jesus came.

Similarly, during this first week of readings in advent, we shall not be focussing so much on the details of Jesus's birth, but on the reason for his coming—that we should all hear God's call to our hearts saying, 'come to me' (Matt 11:28) and that by responding to his call, we should be cleansed from our sins.

The season of Christ's birth provides us with a fresh opportunity to 'come' to him. The call of God is universal, the whole earth is called to listen, yet our response is deeply personal. God is calling to each of us to a personal relationship with himself in Christ. Through that relationship, our lives—which were once lived apart from God—are made new by his presence.

If at first it sounds like a difficult thing for us to do—to listen for the voice of God—thankfully Isaiah points out that matters have been greatly simplified. We can all 'hear the word of the Lord' through the Bible, God's message for humanity. Throughout advent and over the Christmas season, let us not neglect our daily reading of 'the word of the Lord'.

Will you *hear* God's voice as you read his word, and *come* to God, *now*?

> **Prayer:** Lord, thank you that not only at advent, but at all times, you invite us to come to you through your son Jesus. We pray that as we turn our hearts to you, your presence will abide with us throughout our preparations for advent. In Jesus name. Amen.

Advent Reading Plan Day Two: Isaiah 1:10–15; Luke 1:1–4.

Tuesday 5th December: *Wash and Make Yourselves Clean*

> *Wash and make yourselves clean. Take your evil deeds out of my sight; stop doing wrong. Learn to do right; seek justice. Defend the oppressed. Take up the cause of the fatherless; plead the case of the widow. (Isaiah 1:16–17)*

God's reaction to his people's failure is always a call for them to change. Our gracious God provides sinful people (like us!) with an opportunity to repent and amend their ways. Repentance is never futile, for God's call for change is always accompanied by his promise of cleansing—just as a child must first be called to leave playing in the mud before they can have a bath.

God's call to righteousness is both deeply spiritual and intensely practical. It is practical because God calls us to be concerned, as God is, for the oppressed and poor, campaigning for freedom and justice. At the same time, the call is spiritual, for Isaiah understands that it we can only turn away from injustice by drawing near to a just and holy God.

In the Magnificat, Jesus's mother Mary highlights God's concern for the poor and those in need of help:

> *He has brought down rulers from their thrones but has lifted up the humble. He has filled the hungry with good things but has sent the rich away empty. (Luke 1:52–53)*

The message of Christ's birth is the story of God drawing near to his people so that they might be turned from injustice and—by embracing 'the just one'—learn to live in a way which pleases God.

> **Prayer:** Lord, at a time when the world is full of injustice, grant that we your people, in communion with you, may stand up for the rights of the poor and oppressed until we see the justice on earth which your only Son preached and taught. In Jesus name. Amen.

Advent Reading Plan Day Three: Isaiah 1:16–31; Luke 1:5–25.

Wednesday 6th December: *Let us Reason Together*

> *"Come now, and let us reason together," says the Lord, "Though your sins are like scarlet, They shall be as white as snow; Though they are red like crimson, They shall be as wool. (Isaiah 1:18 NKJV)*

God is an intellectual and rational being, and here he actively encourages us to reason with our minds, and to put our intellectual capacities to good use. Since the context of the surrounding verses is a plea to turn from sin and receive forgiveness, God's reasoning runs along these lines:

> *Why refuse to admit your sin, when you can be forgiven?*
>
> *Why continue to live in sin, when you can be made clean?*
>
> *Why live apart from me, when you can know my presence?*

The Christian faith is not a self-help religion—it is a religion which relies heavily on the help of God. The cleansing and forgiveness we need is available freely from the God who longs to cleanse and forgive us. No matter how deep and dark is the stain left by sin. Isaiah uses 'crimson' to speak of sin's guilt as being like a blood stain which will not wash off. Yet God's cleansing is complete: the stains are washed away, the guilt of sin is removed, our consciences are cleansed, and we are given a new moral history—a brand new start.

With its position at the start of the Christian year, advent is the ideal time for us to make a new beginning. God wants us to employ our minds to the question:

> *Why not make a fresh start with God—and why not make it now?*
>
> **Prayer:** Lord, thank you that we can reason together, and that you patiently teach us how to be forgiven and cleansed that we might live for you. We pray to know your cleansing and to walk in your presence today and throughout this advent time. Amen.

Advent Reading Plan Day Four: Isaiah 2; Luke 1:26–38.

Thursday 7th December: *White as Snow*

> *Wash and make yourselves clean. Take your evil deeds out of my sight; stop doing wrong. Learn to do right; seek justice. Defend the oppressed. Take up the cause of the fatherless; plead the case of the widow. (Isaiah 1:16–17)*

The stain of our sin has been removed, so that we are 'as white as snow' – even the pure untouched snow of the highest mountain peaks, the snow in the pre-industrial, pollution free days during which the prophet lived and wrote!

Having cleansed us, God has called us to walk with him, sharing his love of right, and his hatred of wrong. The forgiveness which Christ came to bring makes us born anew, with an unsullied moral profile, that we might share God's love for what is good.

The God who cares for the poor, the fatherless, the refugee, and the widow, calls his people to mirror his concern. Our worship during this advent season will focus on the beauty and majesty of God. But at the same time, we recall that it was not to impress us with his majesty that God stooped to reach out to us in Christ. It was not that we might gaze on him in awe and wonder that he appeared as God made flesh amid the straw of a Bethlehem stable. Instead it was to identify with the poor and the homeless that he was born without the comfortable surroundings of a home. It was to identify with refugees that, when still an infant, he fled to Egypt from the wrath of Herod. It was to show his love for widows that his final instructions from the cross were about the care of his widowed mother. And yet, strangely, because of these things, we see his glory and his beauty magnified even more!

> **Prayer:** We come to you, Lord, preparing our hearts afresh to kneel both at your manger and your throne, with hearts cleansed from sin that we might see and appreciate your unsullied beauty, as is most clearly visible, in your love for us.

Advent Reading Plan Day Five: Isaiah 3; Luke 1:39–56.

Friday 8th December: *Cleansing for Your Heart*

> *If you are willing and obedient, you will eat the good things of the land. (Isaiah 1:19)*

Once God has cleansed our lives and forgiven all our sins, we will experience a complete change of life, with a new willingness to obey God's will. Such obedience is possible, because Christ has broken the power of the sin that once held us captive. Such obedience is also required, because Christ has delivered us to be obedient children.

Of the birth of Jesus, John the Baptist's father Zechariah said:

> *Praise be to the Lord, the God of Israel, because he has come to his people and redeemed them. He has raised up a horn of salvation for us ... to enable us to serve him without fear in holiness and righteousness before him all our days. (Luke 1:68–69, 74–75)*

It is a wonderful thing to be enabled, through Jesus our 'horn of salvation' to be willing to serve God and to obey him. (In the Old Testament, the 'horn' is a symbol of strength, and in the present context speaks the enabling strength which Christ gives us, through his salvation, so that we might live to obey and please God.)

Our obedience brings a great promise with it, too; for when God promises that we 'will eat the good things of the land', he is doing more than promising to provide our daily needs—he is assuring us that we shall experience all his spiritual blessings.

God's word assures us that he has *'blessed us in the heavenly realms with every spiritual blessing in Christ'* (Eph 1:3) and this has been made possible because Jesus has saved us—from our disobedience!

> **Prayer:** Lord, we thank you that Christ has delivered us from sin and disobedience so that we might enjoy the infinite blessing of being obedient to you. Help us always to be willing to hear the voice of God and ready to obey. Amen.

Advent Reading Plan Day Six: Isaiah 4; Luke 1:57–66.

Saturday 9th December: *Cleansing for Your Life*

> *I will thoroughly purge away your dross and remove all your impurities. (1:29)*

At the end of a week of self-examination, as we have considered the call of God for us to repent and find cleansing in his forgiveness, we find the promise of God to 'purge away our dross' and 'remove all our impurities'.

This promise, given at first to God's people Israel, has been extended to all people through the ministry of Christ. It is important to understand that forgiveness, which is a spiritual matter, an unseen transaction between us and God, is accompanied by the visible removal of impurity in everyday life. This translation of the unseen reality of forgiveness into the concrete reality of daily living for God is behind the idea of the Word who was 'made flesh' and who 'dwelt among us'.

The promise of God is that his people will be redeemed with righteousness. Just as this is an important Old Testament theme, it is also important in the New Testament. Christ's righteous act on the cross is what redeems and delivers his penitent people. There are times when examining ourselves we realise our own unworthiness, but we must not allow ourselves to dwell too long on our own shortcomings. Instead, once we have examined ourselves, we are to turn our eyes from our own unrighteousness and unworthiness to our righteous and worthy redeemer. And so, as we prepare to enter the second week of advent, our readings will concentrate on the salvation of God.

> **Prayer:** Lord, we thank you that although your word calls us to understand our own unworthiness, it also turns our eyes toward Jesus, that we might understand how worthy he is to be our saviour and redeemer. In Jesus name. Amen.

Advent Reading Plan Day Seven: Isaiah 5; Luke 1:67–80.

Week 2: Peace on Earth

Sunday 10th December: *Reconciliation*

> *In the last days the mountain of the Lord's temple will be established as the highest of the mountains; it will be exalted above the hills, and all nations will stream to it. (Isaiah 2:2)*

The announcement of the angels to the shepherds of Bethlehem was 'peace on earth, good will to all men.' Until the time of Christ, God had revealed himself almost exclusively to the nation of Israel, but with the coming of Jesus comes a renewed invitation for all nations to come and worship before God. The barrier that blocked human fellowship with God was removed at the cross, and so was the barrier between man and man, and between nation and nation.

When the Gospel writers interpret Isaiah's promise, it is not to the temple but to Jesus, who replaces the temple as the centre of worship, that all nations come. Jew, Greek, Roman and pagan can all approach Israel's God on an equal footing through the beloved son. Common worship leads to common relationship and common interests which make for peace.

This Christian interpretation is not anti-Jewish; such would only be the case if Israel and its people were excluded. On the contrary, not only are they the first to be invited, their invitation still stands. Jesus is born into an idealised Jewish family, and is a model son of the law, but instructs Jew and Gentile alike to obey the law of his God, which is written on his heart.

> **Prayer:** Lord, thank you for the peace Christ has made for us with God, and for the peace he brings between people and nations. Grant as we approach Christmas, that peace shall reign in regions of conflict and of war. Reconcile warring parties, warring nations and even warring families. In Jesus name. Amen.

Advent Reading Plan Day Eight: Isaiah 6; Luke 2:1–7.

Monday 11th December: *Violence Ceases*

> *They will beat their swords into plowshares and their spears into pruning hooks. Nation will not take up sword against nation, nor will they train for war anymore. (Isaiah 2:4)*

It would be a mistake to merely spiritualise or relativize these words. When the peace of Christ enters the human heart, it produces the complete unwillingness to do violence to our fellow men and women; and this in turn leads to the absence of war.

Jesus the Prince of peace never raised an army or carried a weapon. As a child, he fled as a refugee from the jealous anger of Herod, as a young preacher he mildly walked through the hostile crowd that sought to stone him in Nazareth, and on the cross he prayed for his persecutors, saying, 'Father forgive them for they know not what they do.'

To be a follower of Jesus Christ means to cease from violence, and to hope for the day when he will judge between nation and nation, bringing security and peace. At that time, the word of the Angel Gabriel will at last be fulfilled:

> *"The Lord God will give him the throne of his father David, and he will reign over Jacob's descendants forever; his kingdom will never end." (Luke 2:32–33)*

We look forward to the day when peace will reign, because the Prince of peace will reign!

> **Prayer:** Lord, we are too ready to take up arms, to fight for our rights, to kill our enemies. Help us to see the beauty of the hope expressed in your word, that one day we will permanently exchange our weapons of war for implements of peace. Help us to do this in the name of your son, who took the cross, a brutal weapon of Roman torture, and made it a sign of forgiveness and hope. In Jesus name. Amen.

Advent Reading Plan Day Nine: Isaiah 7; Luke 2:8–20.

Tuesday 12th December: *An End of Pride*

> *For all the proud and lofty, for all that is exalted (and they will be humbled) …. The arrogance of man will be brought low and human pride humbled; the Lord alone will be exalted in that day. (Isaiah 2:12, 17)*

This week we are meditating about conflict and its resolution. It is clear that in the majority of cases, whether strife is personal or between nations, it is pride which prevents either side from seeing another's point of view, and seeking a peaceful resolution. That is why we should be both grateful and relieved to hear this promise of God to humble all human pride.

The story of Christ's birth is an object lesson in the humility of our exalted God. The incarnate creator did not choose to be born to a rich or powerful family, but to one which was poor and unknown. He did not come to a palace but to a stable. Mary rejoiced that through his wise and gracious choice:

> *He has performed mighty deeds with his arm; he has scattered those who are proud in their inmost thoughts. He has brought down rulers from their thrones but has lifted up the humble. He has filled the hungry with good things but has sent the rich away empty. (Luke 1:51–53)*

The reconciliation offered by Christ is not merely between people, but between humanity and God. A war of hostility against God's person and will has been constantly raging since it began in the Garden of Eden. But the coming of Christ at Christmas announces its end.

> **Prayer:** Lord, thank you for the peace Christ has made for us with God, and for the peace he brings between people and nations. Grant that as we approach Christmas, peace shall reign in regions of conflict and war. Reconcile warring parties, nations, and even warring families. In Jesus name. Amen.

Advent Reading Plan Day Ten: Isaiah 8; Luke 2:21–35.

Wednesday 13th December: *The Glory of God*

And they were calling to one another: "Holy, holy, holy is the Lord Almighty; the whole earth is full of his glory." (Isaiah 6:3)

At this present time, large parts of the world are filled with violence, and news of inhuman acts fill our newspapers and television screens. Since the end of hostilities in the Second World War, there has not been a single day in which war has not continued somewhere on the planet.

The world of Isaiah's day was also experiencing the scourge of war, due to the ruthless expansion of the Assyrian empire. Yet Isaiah had hope both for the present and the future. Today we will consider his present hope, and tomorrow his future hope.

In chapter 6, above all the strife of the world, Isaiah sees a vision of God, exalted on his throne, worshipped by powerful angels. These angels continually cry that God is holy: whether in times of war or peace, he is beyond the wickedness and sin which pollutes our world, and even now he is reigning.

The whole earth is—at this present time—full of God's glory as seen in creation. If men took time to look up from their guns, they would glimpse the beautiful heavens, the grandeur of the mountains and rivers, the delicate beauty of the butterfly. For me, one of the most iconic moments in cinema occurs in Gladiator, when after the carnage of war, director Ridley Scot pans out to a scene of a robin singing in the snow, for me a depiction of the whole of creation crying out to humanity: stop the violence, be still, and behold God's glory!

> **Prayer:** Lord, we thank you that although the earth is full of violence, you sit above the strife, speaking words of peace, love and reconciliation for the world. At this advent season, grant that we may be still to hear the angels singing 'holy, holy, holy, is the Lord Almighty: the whole earth is full of his glory'. In Jesus name. Amen.

Advent Reading Plan Day Eleven: Isaiah 9; Luke 2:36–40.

Thursday 14th December: *The Glory of God Yet to Come*

> *For the earth will be filled with the knowledge of the Lord as the waters cover the sea. (Isaiah 11:9)*

If Isaiah could take hope in God's unassailable glory revealed in the present, he could also hope for a future day when that same glory, in an inexpressible measure, would flood the world. This hope of God's glory filling the earth with the atmosphere of heaven is a major theme in Isaiah, bound up with the hope of the coming messiah. The messianic age is the time when the glory of God will fill the earth. Christ revealed God's glory through his miracles of compassion and healing; he further revealed God's glory through his death and resurrection; but his glory shall only be fully and finally revealed when Christ comes again. At that time:

> *The wolf will live with the lamb, the leopard will lie down with the goat, the calf and the lion and the yearling together; and a little child will lead them. The cow will feed with the bear, their young will lie down together, and the lion will eat straw like the ox. The infant will play near the cobra's den, the young child will put its hand into the viper's nest. They will neither harm nor destroy on all my holy mountain, for the earth will be filled with the knowledge of the Lord as the waters cover the sea. (Isaiah 11:6–9)*

Isaiah's vision links Christ's coming with the restoration of creation, and, as the angels announced over the fields of Bethlehem, peace on earth. Christ's work of bringing peace began the moment he was born, continued through his life, and will be completed when he comes 'on the clouds of heaven in power and in great glory' (Matt 24:30).

> **Prayer:** Lord, we praise you for the blessed hope that your coming again in glory will mean the restoration of creation, and the dawning of a reign of peace on earth. Grant as we await your coming glory, we shall do all we can to promote 'peace on earth, and good will to all'. In Jesus name. Amen.

Advent Reading Plan Day Twelve: Isaiah 10; Luke 2:41–52.

Friday 15th December: *All Flesh Shall See the Glory of God*

"And the glory of the Lord will be revealed, and all people will see it together. For the mouth of the Lord has spoken." (Isaiah 40:5)

Saint Luke takes up this theme of a worldwide salvation; all flesh is an inclusive term, and Luke favours inclusion. The prophecy is fulfilled by the revelation of Jesus through the ministry of John the Baptist. Luke links Isaiah 40:5 with Isaiah 49:6 to show that the glory of God was bound up with a person, the one who brings salvation.

"A voice of one calling in the wilderness, 'Prepare the way for the Lord … And all people will see God's salvation.'" (Luke 3:4–6)

Beginning with his own Jewish people, Jesus brings a salvation which will eventually impact the whole earth, every tribe and nation will bow before God, and rejoice in his salvation.

In case there should be any misunderstanding about the universal, unconditional message of salvation, Isaiah tells us that those who rejected this message would, in effect, exclude themselves. Luke is similarly clear that only those who obey the gospel message can receive the salvation which God offers to all people. Why is this? It is because salvation is bound up with a person, Jesus, and to welcome him is to welcome the salvation of God. That is why Luke records Simeon in the temple, taking the infant Jesus in his arms to say:

"Sovereign Lord, as you have promised, you may now dismiss your servant in peace. For my eyes have seen your salvation." (Luke 2:29–30)

To take Jesus as our Saviour is to receive God's salvation.

Prayer: Lord, as you have promised, we are now able (whenever the time comes) to depart his world in peace, for we have received your salvation in Jesus—who has made peace between us and you forever. In Jesus name. Amen.

Advent Reading Plan Day Thirteen: Isaiah 11; Luke 3:1–6.

Saturday 16th December: *Who Will Go For Us?*

> *In the year that King Uzziah died, I saw the Lord, high and exalted, seated on a throne; and the train of his robe filled the temple. ... Then I heard the voice of the Lord saying, "Whom shall I send? And who will go for us?" And I said, "Here am I. Send me!" (Isaiah 6:1, 8)*

It was when Isaiah heard and responded to God's voice that he volunteered for service. First came the revelation of the glory and holiness of God, then came the call for someone, in response to God's revealed character, to surrender their lives to him in service. God is always our *first cause*: he takes the initiative in revealing himself to our hearts and in calling us to serve him.

Jesus came into the world to bring a fuller revelation of the glory of God than Isaiah could have imagined. Even though Jesus, God's Son, shared God's nature, he said, 'I have not come to be served but to serve' and declared his motivation in so doing 'I always do those things which please my Father' (Matt 20:28; John 8:29).

As we go about our busy schedules at this time of year, let us not forget the reason for our service, or the focus of our devotion. We have seen his glory, we have heard his call, and we have responded, 'here am I send me'.

Many will be busy serving others over Christmas: in church services, homeless shelters, soup kitchens, nursing homes, hospitals and in countless other ways. If we share the motive of Jesus and Isaiah, then every act of love and compassion to our fellow humans is an act of worship and devotion to our God.

> **Prayer:** Lord, help us to mirror your servant heart, so that at this very busy time of year, we shall focus our attention not only on the people whom we serve, but on the God who has called us to serve him and humanity.

Advent Reading Plan Day Fourteen: Isaiah 12; Matt 1:1–17.

Week 3: Serving the Lord

Sunday 17th December: *His Name Shall be Immanuel*

> *Therefore the Lord himself will give you a sign: The virgin will conceive and give birth to a son, and will call him Immanuel. (Isaiah 7:14)*

The birth of Christ is foreshadowed by the birth of a child whom the prophet names Immanuel, 'God with us.' As we go about our service, we remember not only that we are doing it *for* God, but also *with* God.

God is still concerned for the needs of humanity, and according to Jesus he is always actively at work on their behalf (John 5:17). God incarnate walked dusty roads to help the weak and heal the sick, he sat on a hillside to teach the hungry hearts of those who found spiritual satisfaction through his gospel; he knelt down and rolled up his sleeves to wash dirt from the feet of his disciples. This is our God, the servant king. Every time we help the poor with food or shelter, welcome the refugee, offer advice to the young, teach people the glorious message of Christmas, we are not doing it alone—we are doing it with God, as his fellow workers.

Where is God? He is behind us and in front of us—he is at the right and the left of us. He is all these things, for he is with us and in us.

As we enter the third week of advent, Christmas is very close. Our schedule may be tiring, the demands on our time and energy may great. But God with us promises to give us all the help and strength we need to serve him and others.

> **Prayer:** Dear God, please help me to realise that as I fit my Christian service in to an already busy work and family schedule, I am not alone, and I am not serving merely in my own strength, for you are with me to strengthen and support me in my work. In Jesus name. Amen.

Advent Reading Plan Day Fifteen: Isaiah 40; Matt 1:18–25.

Monday 18th December: *Wonderful Counsellor*

> *For to us a child is born, to us a son is given, and the government will be on his shoulders. And he will be called Wonderful Counsellor, Mighty God, Everlasting Father, Prince of Peace. (Isaiah 9:6)*

The child to be born is the wonderful counsellor. When the word wonderful was used in the Old Testament, it denoted an 'other-worldly' nature, a heavenly reality, as when the angel of the Lord spoke to Manoah 'why do you ask my name, seeing it is wonderful?' (Judges 13:18 NKJV). Christ's advice for our lives (his counsel) is wonderful because it comes from a superior and heavenly source.

His wisdom is from above, and so is 'pure ... peace-loving, considerate, submissive, full of mercy and good fruit, impartial and sincere' (James 3:17).

It is true that most of our plans for Christmas were made long before advent. Even so, perhaps today many decisions will need to be made, and this is true throughout the year, not just at special times. The Bible does not promise us simple answers to life's pressing questions, or dreams from heaven to guide us, but God nevertheless promises to guide his people: 'The Lord will guide you always' (Isaiah 58:11). It is by Christ's own wisdom, often undetected by us, that he guides and leads his people.

The whole world mobilised that Jesus might be born in Bethlehem—his parents could not have arranged that. A new star in the sky to lead the wise men—no scientist could have created it. The angel choir over Bethlehem was not commissioned by any artistic director. Only God could have guided the events of the first Christmas—by his wisdom.

> **Prayer:** Lord, we are not always sure of your leading and guidance. Help us to accept the assurance that you are leading and guiding us throughout life, so that we may live for your glory; and when life ends, you will lead us to fountains of living water, where your glory may be seen. Amen

Advent Reading Plan Day Sixteen: Isaiah 41; Matt 2:1–12.

Tuesday 19th December: *A Shoot from the Stump of Jesse*

> A shoot will come up from the stump of Jesse; from his roots a Branch will bear fruit. The Spirit of the Lord will rest on him—the Spirit of wisdom and of understanding, the Spirit of counsel and of might, the Spirit of the knowledge and fear of the Lord—and he will delight in the fear of the Lord. (Isaiah 11:1)

At this time of year perhaps more than any other, the church asks itself, 'what can we do to make a real difference on our world and community?' We feel so ineffective to make a difference and to lead others into the worship of the Living God.

In the verse above, Isaiah assures the people that after a long absence of a Davidic king, the Christ (a descendent of David) would come to them, and would be anointed with the Spirit of wisdom and understanding. Though we may not know the way into people's hearts, or appreciate how to make an effective difference in their lives, this wise king does. It is as we follow Christ and obey his word, that we put his wisdom, not ours, into practise.

As we proclaim Christ at Christmas we are sharing the formerly hidden, yet now revealed, mystery of God's wise plan for humanity. Jesus came into this world to fulfil God's rescue mission for all people, to provide a homecoming for the wander, forgiveness for the sinner, peace for the troubled heart, and a new start for the repentant.

Our message remains as relevant in the twenty first century as it was in the first, and ever shall be.

> **Prayer:** Lord, as your servants called to proclaim the good news of Christ to all people, help us to be freshly inspired by, and freshly assured of, the unchanging relevance of your message for all humanity, that it represents your wisdom and understanding—your perfect and undiluted answer for a sin sick world. In Jesus name. Amen.

Advent Reading Plan Day Seventeen: Isaiah 42; Matt 2:13–18.

Wednesday 20th December: *The Joy of Our Salvation*

With joy you will draw water from the wells of salvation. (Isaiah 12:3)

Not everyone loves this time of year. And even for many of us, Christmas remains tinged with sadness because of the absence of loved ones, or because of loneliness when we have no one to share our Christmas with. I have experienced both these feelings and worse at Christmas time. And yet I still love Christmas and advent.

As we reach out beyond ourselves to serve God this year, we find a source of joy that runs deeper than our own emotions and beyond life's sad experiences. Our joy springs like a pure fountain from a well so deep that it is beyond whatever harm this world may throw at us. It is the well of salvation, which the Bible says is not located deep down in the earth, but deep in our hearts. The secret of this well is that it connects to an upper spring, which reaches all the way to heaven, and to Christ himself, the source of our life and joy.

As we endeavour to serve others, or to be a witness for Christ, at this Christmas season, we will find a source of joy which is entirely outside of ourselves, and yet it springs ups within us. Jesus is the source of joy! It is not make-believe; it is not a vain effort to lift our own hearts out of the doldrums! It is a strong, sustaining presence of the God who deeply cares about our pain and in whose presence is fullness of joy. If you've been hurt at Christmas, perhaps this year the Lord will lead you to someone just as bitterly bruised: they may need to know how you got through. Don't be afraid. Share your joy.

> **Prayer:** Lord, I admit that sometimes I find Christmas difficult. My sorrow wells up inside me. Please grant that your joy shall also spring up, comforting and consoling, that I might be open to share the blessings you have given me with others, and perhaps even make some new friends this year. In Jesus name. Amen

Advent Reading Plan Day Eighteen: Isaiah 43; Matt 2:19–23.

Thursday 21ˢᵗ December: *The Government on His Shoulders*

For to us a child is born, to us a son is given, and the government will be on his shoulders. And he will be called Wonderful Counsellor, Mighty God, Everlasting Father, Prince of Peace. (Isaiah 9:6)

Are you carrying a heavy burden of service this Christmas? Perhaps you are engaged in ministry, and the spiritual needs of the people are on your mind. Perhaps you are cooking Christmas dinner for the family, or for the homeless, and you are longing for the help of the one who fed the 5,000!

In every area of his people's lives, Jesus carries the weight of responsibility for us as our leader, friend, and guide. From the highest political leaders, and the most prominent church leaders, who have responsibility for many, to the lowliest of us in our homes, concerned only for our families and local parish churches, Christ carries the burdens of his people on his shoulders.

History shows that if proud rulers humble themselves, God will hear and answer them (think of Nebuchadnezzar in Daniel 4). If religious leaders seek him he will be found. If the lowly turn to him, he will not despise their plea but grant them justice, mercy, and a place near him among the most honoured of men and women. Our leader is the Lord of all, from the highest of kings to the lowest of servants, because the king of glory became the lowliest of all that he might redeem us.

If it's entertainment you're looking for, trust the TV guide. But if you are grappling with the problems of real life, Jesus is still the one you need. When it comes to the help we need for life, Christ wins the top ratings every year, he's always the Christmas number one.

> **Prayer:** We thank you, O Lord, that whatever human authority may rule the land in which we live, and whatever burdens we may bear, ultimately the government of the whole world is, and ever shall be, on your shoulders. Amen.

Advent Reading Plan Day Eighteen: Isaiah 44; John 1:1–5.

Friday 22nd December: *The Light of God*

> *The people walking in darkness have seen a great light; on those living in the land of deep darkness a light has dawned. You have enlarged the nation and increased their joy; they rejoice before you as people rejoice at the harvest (Isaiah 9:2–3)*

As we prepare to celebrate Christ's coming into the world, we find the familiar theme of light displacing darkness. Jesus, 'the light of the world,' was born to redeem humanity from the darkness of sin. What we are not so familiar with is the image of people celebrating harvest festival, right in the middle of our advent text! Surely, here is a verse we can save for autumn for the harvest festival service?!

But no. The image is in its correct place as part of our advent celebrations. The images of light and darkness, although powerful, may seem somewhat abstract, but this is not the prophet's intention. His illustrations are based on concrete realities. The picture is of prisoners of war, or perhaps slaves, kept in a dungeon without light, being set free and walking out into the sunlight. The same is true for the picture of harvest. Imagine the rejoicing of those who, being long without enough food, receive a harvest sufficient for themselves and their families!

The gospel of Jesus brings this reality home to us, for though it initially has more to do with our souls than our stomachs, the sensation of being full, or abundantly satisfied in God, is just as real. Then, once our souls are satisfied with God, we find that we are also filled with God's own compassion for the poor and hungry, so that we may join him in working to meet the needs of their poverty.

> **Prayer:** Lord, as you have satisfied the longing of our hearts to be filled with you, so help us to work together to eradicate the poverty which brings hunger to the poor of our world. Grant that the fulness of Christ in our hearts will lead us to fill the emptiness of the hungry—both spiritually and materially. In Jesus name. Amen.

Advent Reading Plan Day Nineteen: Isaiah 45; John 1:6–13.

Saturday 23rd December: *God my Salvation*

Surely God is my salvation; I will trust and not be afraid. The Lord, the Lord himself, is my strength and my defense; he has become my salvation." (Isaiah 12:2)

We cannot tell others of God's wonderful salvation until we have experienced it for ourselves. This is the message of the verse above us. As Isaiah declared the salvation of God to others, he did so from personal experience: 'God is my salvation ... my defence'.

It is reassuring that as we set out to worship and serve God throughout the Christmas season, his plan is that we should have a personal encounter with him, so that we might share the blessings which we receive from that encounter with others.

When the shepherds came to Bethlehem, in response to the message of the angel, they encountered Christ for themselves. They told Mary and Joseph about what the angel had said, and as they left the scene, and probably for many days afterward, they told everyone they met about the remarkable events of that first Christmas night.

Having once encountered God as our Saviour, we are motivated to share him with others. Church evangelism is not a cynical or narrow-minded programme which exists solely that we may convert others to our own point of view. Rather, it is the activity of a once hungry, but now satisfied soul, who wants to share what he/she has received with others. When I lived in Cardiff, I befriended a group of homeless people. If a meal was on offer at the Salvation Army soup kitchen, or a bed for the night was free at the shelter, they were always keen to tell other homeless people about it, and pass on the good news.

Having experienced so much from God, let's not be mean! Pass it on!

> **Prayer:** God my Saviour, as you have blessed my life with your strength hand deliverance, help me to bless others by telling them how they too may know you as their salvation. In Jesus name. Amen.

Advent Reading Plan Day Twenty: Isaiah 46; John 1:14–18.

Week 4: Worship and Waiting

Sunday 24th December: *Songs of Praise*

> *Give praise to the Lord, proclaim his name; make known among the nations what he has done, and proclaim that his name is exalted. Sing to the Lord, for he has done glorious things; let this be known to all the world. Shout aloud and sing for joy, people of Zion, for great is the Holy One of Israel among you. (Isaiah 12:4–6)*

This year, the last Sunday in advent is the day before Christmas Day. And if we have only one day left, we need to spend it wisely, organising our time to do only the most essential things.

There is one thing which is essential: as we welcome Christ's coming into the world, we must bring to him our gifts of praise and thanksgiving. Sounds of joy and happiness are fitting at this time of year, and especially so when they are directed towards God in worship. For God has done 'glorious things', taking on himself the form of man, born as a baby in Bethlehem, that he might become our Saviour. Isaiah sees the manifestation of God's presence as cause to shout and sing for joy. The presence of God brings an exuberance into our worship—Christ has come, God is really among us! Let's get excited!

After all, births are joyous occasions. Tomorrow, many of us will celebrate by giving presents, perhaps eating a little too much, and by spending time with family. Even those who are working on the big day will find some time for this over the Christmas season. But what of today? Let's make it a day to shout and sing our praises, for Jesus our king has come, and 'great is the Holy One of Israel' among us!

> **Prayer:** Lord, as Isaiah praised you for the good news of Christ and the great things you have done, so we would praise you at this Christmas season for bringing your only son Jesus into the world, to save us from our sins. Hallelujah! Amen.

Advent Reading Plan Day One: Isaiah 47; Galatians 4:1–7.

Christmas Day: *Renew Your Strength*

> *But those who hope in the LORD will renew their strength. They will soar on wings like eagles; they will run and not grow weary, they will walk and not be faint. (Isaiah 40:31)*

Christmas Day has finally arrived, and although it is a time of great joy, for some it can also be a time of hard work and stress. If this is true for you, then take courage form the verse above.

Jesus was born into this world, and following his death and resurrection, he returned to heaven. From there, he has sent his Spirit to abide with his people always, so that we are never without God's presence. On this Christmas Day, we can focus on the reality of God's presence with us in everything we do.

Some will be at work today, in hospitals, in the service industry, or in the emergency services. Many of us will be engaged in church services, leading worship, or providing food and shelter for the poor through our church programmes. Others will be glad of an afternoon off to sit in front of the television. But wherever we find ourselves today, God's presence will never leave us.

Let's take time to appreciate, and not ignore, God's presence today, for in God's presence, our strength is renewed. When we are called upon to expend our energy in any task, we will not grow faint or weary, whether the tasks are hard ('they will run and not grow weary') or easy ('they will walk and not be faint').

Whatever you are doing today, *God with us* shall make all the difference in your life. May you blessed with his presence!

> **Prayer:** Lord, we praise you for the glory of Christmas—that God is with us, and will never leave us. As we go into this day, facing joys and sorrows, blessings and challenges, may we know the presence of God who will renew or strength that we may 'soar on wings like eagles.' In Jesus name. Amen.

Advent Reading Plan Day One: Isaiah 48; 1 Tim 3:16.

www.ingramcontent.com/pod-product-compliance
Lightning Source LLC
Chambersburg PA
CBHW061317040426
42444CB00010B/2686